Dreams
Colouring
Book

Dreams
Colouring
Book

ARCTURUS

This edition published in 2019 by Arcturus Publishing Limited
26/27 Bickels Yard, 151–153 Bermondsey Street,
London SE1 3HA

Copyright © Arcturus Holdings Limited

ISBN: 978-1-78950-161-2
CH007045NT
Supplier 29, Date 0519, Print Run 8971

Printed in China

Created for children 10+

Introduction

The *Dreams Colouring Book* unlocks a rich, fascinating world of imaginative play and demonstrates that you don't have to be asleep to dream. The delightful collection of black and white images includes fairy tale castles, unicorns, mermaids, magical moons, beautiful angels and phantasmagorical abstracts. Complete the pictures in colours of your choice; even use them to inspire your own original dream art.

What better way to illustrate your unconscious thoughts than with colouring, a pastime that has been shown to enhance creativity and aid concentration? The *Dreams Colouring Book* presents an art challenge that will bring a sense of calm and encourage self-expression.

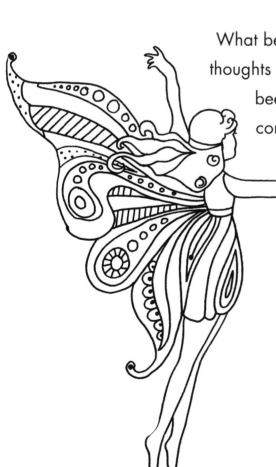

Bethany

Bethany

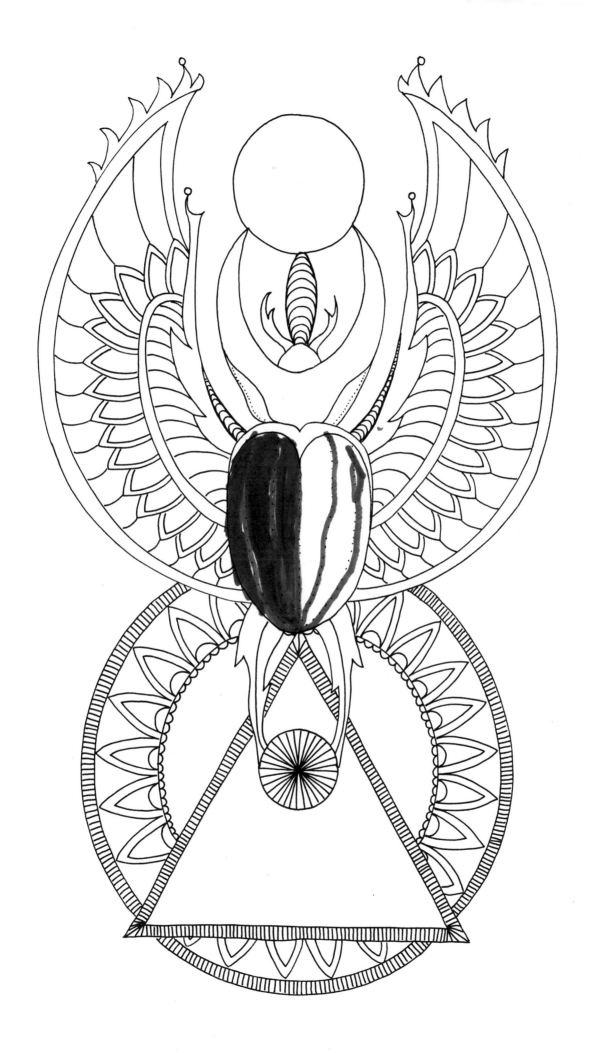

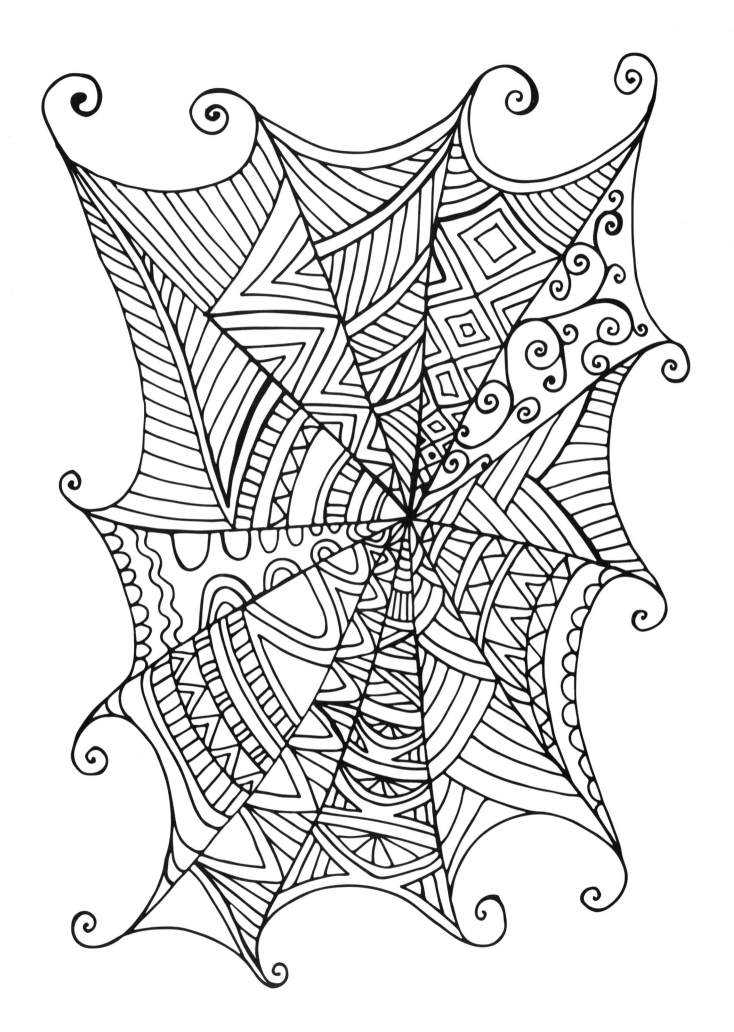

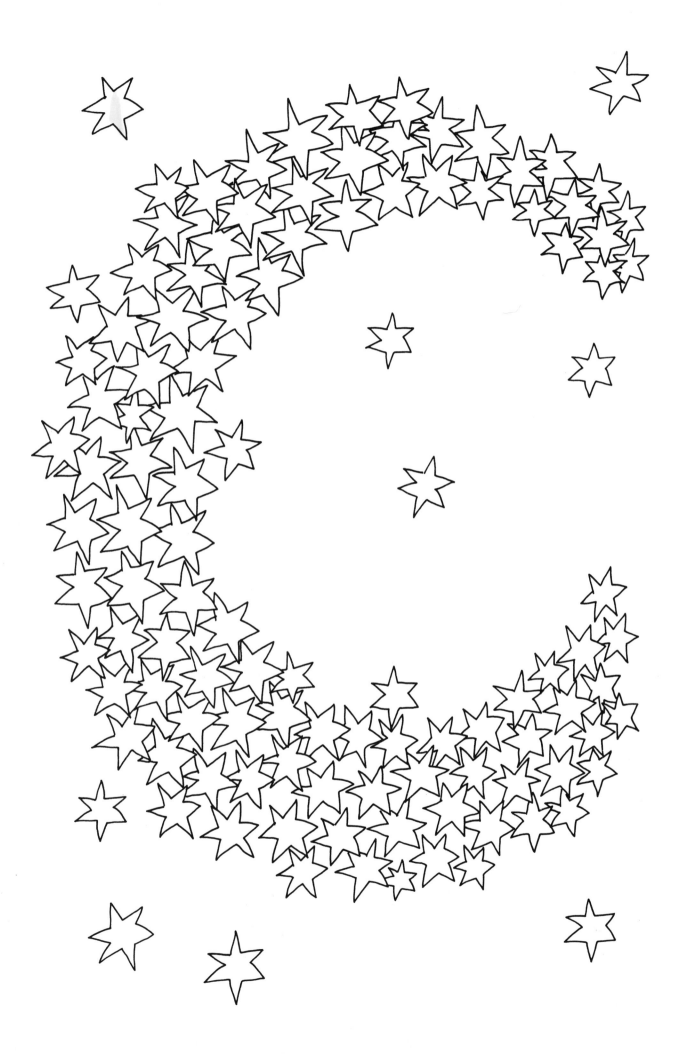

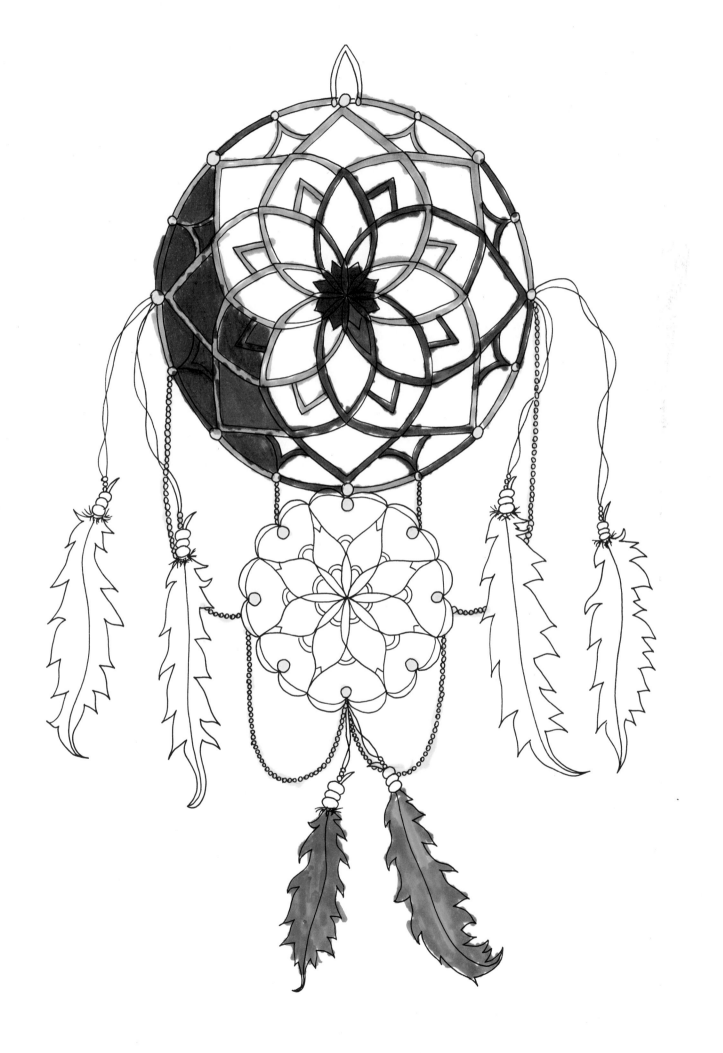

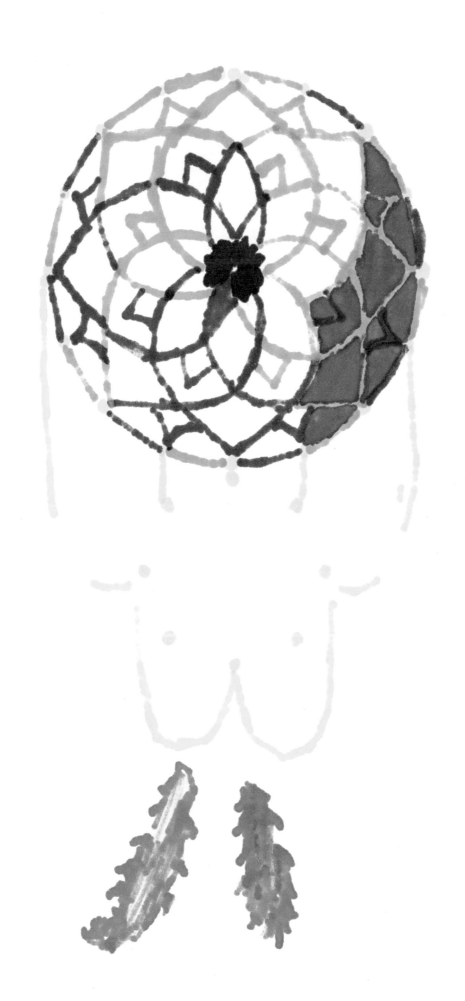

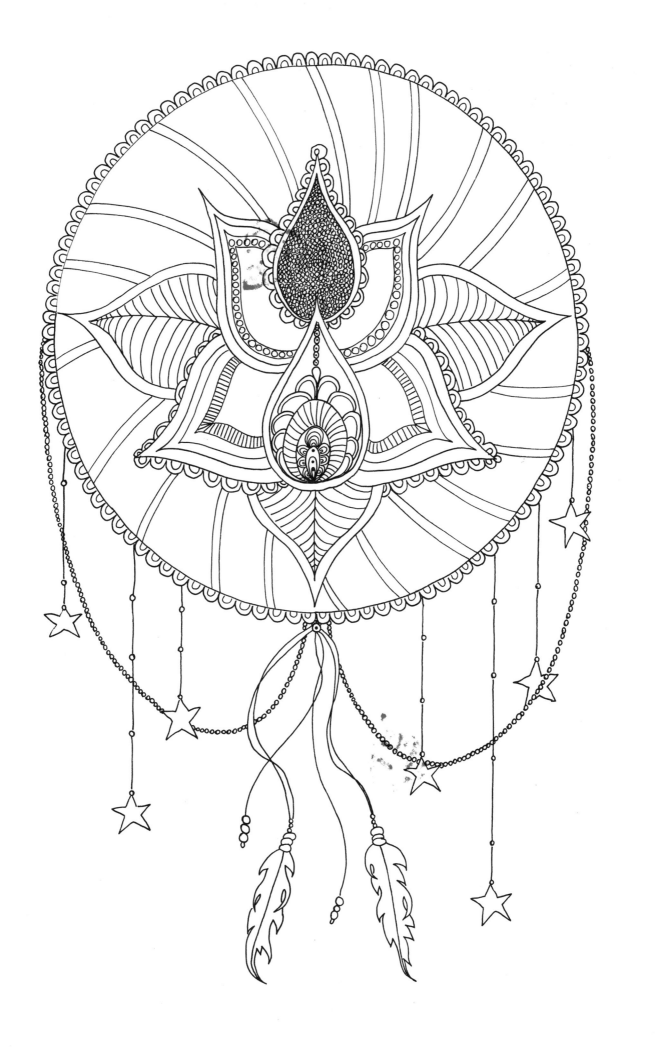